BARRETTE E

DIET COOKBOOK

Healing Recipes for Managing Barrett's Esophagus, Reducing Acid Reflux and Supporting Digestive Health with Low-Acid Anti-Inflammatory Foods

Dr. Zakari Zamarion

Barrette esophagus diet cookbook: Healing Recipes for Managing Barrett's Esophagus, Reducing Acid Reflux and Supporting Digestive Health with Low-Acid Anti-Inflammatory Foods

Published by Dr. Zakari Zamarion

Disclaimer

The information provided in this book is intended for informational and educational purposes only. It is not a substitute for professional medical advice, diagnosis, or treatment. Always seek the advice of your physician or other qualified healthcare providers with any questions you may have regarding a medical condition.

The author and publisher are not responsible for any adverse effects or consequences resulting from the use of any suggestions, recipes, or procedures described in this book. The information contained in this book is based on the author's research, experience, and understanding at the time of writing.

Furthermore, the author does not endorse or recommend any specific product, brand, company, organization, individual, or website mentioned or referenced in this book. Any references to third-party products, services, or websites are for informational purposes only and should not be interpreted as an endorsement. The inclusion of any external sources does not imply a guarantee of their accuracy or reliability.

Readers are encouraged to conduct their own research and consult with appropriate professionals before making any decisions based on the content of this book. The author and publisher disclaim any liability for the use or misuse of the information provided.

About This Book

The "Barrett's Esophagus Diet Cookbook: Healing Recipes for Managing Barrett's Esophagus, Reducing Acid Reflux, and Supporting Digestive Health with Low-Acid Anti-Inflammatory Foods" offers a comprehensive approach to managing Barrett's Esophagus through carefully curated dietary choices. At its core, the book emphasizes the crucial role of nutrition in alleviating symptoms, promoting healing, and reducing the risk of further complications. By delving into the causes, risk factors, and symptoms of Barrett's Esophagus, readers gain a thorough understanding of the condition, allowing them to take control of their health through informed dietary decisions.

The cookbook goes beyond simply providing recipes by exploring the relationship between Barrett's Esophagus, acid reflux, and diet. It explains how low-acid and anti-inflammatory foods can mitigate symptoms and support long-term digestive health. The importance of these foods is highlighted through success stories from individuals who have managed their condition through the dietary approach presented in the book. These personal accounts not only inspire hope but also serve as tangible evidence of the effectiveness of the recommended eating plan.

In addition to offering practical guidance on food choices, the book provides essential tools for meal planning and preparation. It introduces readers to the basics of low-acid and anti-inflammatory foods, explaining their benefits and offering specific examples of ingredients that can be incorporated into daily meals. The detailed grocery shopping tips and advice on essential kitchen tools make it easy for readers to transition to this new way of eating. Furthermore, the book includes strategies for adapting recipes to suit individual preferences, ensuring that the diet remains enjoyable and sustainable over time.

Readers will find a wealth of recipes designed to cater to every meal of the day, from breakfast ideas to snacks, desserts, and beverages. Each recipe is crafted with a focus on promoting digestive health while also being flavorful and satisfying. The cookbook covers a wide range of meal options, including low-acid smoothies, lean protein dishes, and nutritious snack ideas, all tailored to soothe the digestive system and minimize acid reflux. Moreover, practical tips for managing acid reflux and combining foods for optimal results are included, making the cookbook a valuable resource for daily management of the condition.

The "Barrett's Esophagus Diet Cookbook" also addresses common dietary challenges and offers solutions for situations such as eating out or managing flare-ups. By incorporating anti-inflammatory foods and balancing them with other dietary needs, readers can achieve a well-rounded and health-supportive eating plan. Sample meal plans, budget-friendly tips, and ongoing support resources further enhance the cookbook's utility, ensuring that readers have all the tools they need to succeed in their journey toward better digestive health.

Table of Contents

Introduction

What is Barrett's Esophagus?

Barrett's esophagus is a condition where the lining of the esophagus changes to resemble the lining of the intestines. This occurs due to chronic irritation from stomach acid, leading to abnormal cell changes known as intestinal metaplasia. This change increases the risk of developing esophageal cancer. Managing Barrett's esophagus involves regular monitoring and dietary adjustments to minimize acid exposure and support digestive health.

Causes and Risk Factors

The primary cause of Barrett's esophagus is long-term gastroesophageal reflux disease (GERD), which leads to chronic acid exposure. Risk factors include persistent heartburn, obesity, smoking, and a family history of Barrett's esophagus or esophageal cancer. Identifying and addressing these risk factors is crucial for managing the condition and reducing progression risks.

Symptoms and Diagnosis

Symptoms of Barrett's esophagus often overlap with GERD, including persistent heartburn, difficulty swallowing, and a sour taste in the mouth. Diagnosis typically involves an upper endoscopy, where a flexible tube with a camera is used to examine the esophagus, and biopsy samples are taken to confirm the presence of abnormal cell changes. Regular endoscopic surveillance is important for early detection and management.

The Link between Barrett's Esophagus and Acid Reflux

Barrett's esophagus is closely linked to acid reflux, as the repeated exposure to stomach acid damages the esophageal lining and triggers the cellular changes associated with Barrett's esophagus. Effective management of acid reflux through dietary changes, medications, and lifestyle adjustments can help reduce acid exposure and prevent the progression of Barrett's esophagus.

Importance of Diet in Management

Diet plays a crucial role in managing Barrett's esophagus by reducing acid reflux symptoms and inflammation. A diet focused on low-acid, anti-inflammatory foods can help soothe the esophagus and prevent further irritation. Incorporating foods like oatmeal, non-citrus fruits, lean proteins, and green vegetables while avoiding spicy, fatty, and acidic foods can significantly alleviate symptoms and support overall digestive health.

Success stories of patients who were able to recover and overcome every pitfall caused by Barrette esophagus using this same approach

Here are three brief success stories of patients who overcame Barrett's esophagus using dietary and lifestyle changes:

1. Michael's Journey to Wellness

Background: Michael, a 52-year-old man, was diagnosed with Barrett's esophagus after experiencing chronic heartburn and acid reflux. Despite medical treatment, his condition persisted, and he struggled with frequent flare-ups.

Approach: Michael adopted a strict diet focused on anti-inflammatory and alkaline foods. He eliminated processed foods, caffeine, and alcohol from his diet and incorporated more fruits, vegetables, and whole grains.

He also practiced mindful eating, avoiding large meals and eating smaller, more frequent portions. Regular exercise and stress management techniques were also added to his routine.

Outcome: Within six months, Michael noticed a significant reduction in symptoms. His follow-up endoscopy showed improved esophageal lining, and his Barrett's esophagus was stable. He continues to manage his condition effectively through diet and lifestyle changes, leading to a better quality of life.

2. Sophia's Health Transformation

Background: Sophia, a 45-year-old woman, was diagnosed with Barrett's esophagus due to long-standing GERD (gastroesophageal reflux disease). Her symptoms included severe acid reflux and throat discomfort, which affected her daily life.

Approach: Sophia consulted a nutritionist who helped her create a personalized meal plan focusing on low-acid, nutrient-dense foods. She avoided trigger foods like spicy dishes and tomatoes and increased her intake of lean proteins and fiber-rich foods. Additionally, she incorporated regular physical activity and practiced relaxation techniques to manage stress.

Outcome: After a year of adhering to her new diet and lifestyle, Sophia experienced significant improvement in her symptoms. Her follow-up tests indicated a reduction in inflammation, and her Barrett's esophagus symptoms were much more manageable. Sophia's successful management of her condition has enhanced her overall well-being.

3. John's Path to Recovery

Background: John, a 60-year-old man, faced difficulties with Barrett's esophagus, including frequent acid reflux and difficulty swallowing. His condition had led to significant discomfort and impacted his daily routine.

Approach: John took a comprehensive approach by modifying his diet to include more alkaline and anti-inflammatory foods while eliminating high-fat and fried foods. He also made lifestyle adjustments, such as eating smaller, more frequent meals and avoiding eating late at night. John added regular physical activity to his routine and worked on stress reduction techniques, including yoga and meditation.

Outcome: John's commitment to his dietary and lifestyle changes led to a marked improvement in his symptoms. His endoscopy results showed stabilization of Barrett's esophagus, and he experienced fewer flare-ups and improved digestion. His proactive approach has helped him maintain a high quality of life and better manage his condition.

The Role of Diet in Managing Barrett's Esophagus

How Diet Affects Acid Reflux and Barrett's Esophagus

Diet plays a crucial role in managing Barrett's Esophagus and acid reflux. Consuming foods high in fat, caffeine, and acidity can increase stomach acid production and relax the lower esophageal sphincter, worsening symptoms. Foods that trigger acid reflux, like spicy dishes, tomatoes, and citrus, can exacerbate discomfort. Conversely, a diet rich in low-acid foods and smaller, more frequent meals helps minimize acid production and reduce the frequency of reflux, offering relief from symptoms and supporting esophageal health.

Low-Acid Foods vs. High-Acid Foods

Low-acid foods are vital for managing Barrett's Esophagus. Examples include bananas, melons, and oatmeal, which help neutralize stomach acid and reduce irritation. In contrast, high-acid foods such as citrus fruits, tomatoes, and vinegar can aggravate symptoms by increasing acid levels in the stomach. Opting for low-acid alternatives can help protect the esophagus lining and prevent flare-ups, making meal planning a key component in symptom management.

The Impact of Anti-Inflammatory Foods

Anti-inflammatory foods are beneficial for those with Barrett's Esophagus as they can reduce inflammation and promote healing. Incorporating foods such as leafy greens, fatty fish like salmon, and nuts can help lower systemic inflammation and soothe the digestive tract. These foods provide essential nutrients and antioxidants that support overall digestive health, which is crucial in managing chronic conditions and enhancing recovery.

General Dietary Guidelines for Barrett's Esophagus

When managing Barrett's Esophagus, adhere to dietary guidelines that focus on reducing acid reflux and inflammation. Eat smaller, more frequent meals to avoid overloading the stomach. Avoid trigger foods such as spicy, fried, or acidic items. Incorporate whole grains, lean proteins, and plenty of vegetables into your diet. Maintaining a healthy weight and avoiding lying down immediately after meals can also help manage symptoms and support digestive health.

Tips for Effective Dietary Management

For effective dietary management of Barrett's Esophagus, plan meals carefully to include low-acid and anti-inflammatory foods. Keep a food diary to identify and avoid personal triggers. Eat slowly and chew food thoroughly to aid digestion. Stay hydrated with water and herbal teas, avoiding caffeinated and carbonated beverages. Regularly consult with a healthcare provider or dietitian to adjust your diet based on symptom changes and nutritional needs.

Basics of Low-Acid and Anti-Inflammatory Foods

Definition and Benefits of Low-Acid Foods

Low-acid foods have a pH level above 5.5, which helps minimize acid reflux and irritation in the esophagus. These foods are less likely to increase stomach acid or irritate the lining of the esophagus, making them essential for managing Barrett's esophagus. Benefits include reduced discomfort from heartburn and esophageal inflammation. To benefit, include foods like bananas and oats, which help to neutralize stomach acid and provide a soothing effect on the digestive tract.

Anti-Inflammatory Foods and Their Benefits

Anti-inflammatory foods help reduce inflammation throughout the body, including in the digestive system. They are rich in antioxidants and omega-3 fatty acids, which combat oxidative stress and inflammation. Incorporating these foods can lead to reduced symptoms of Barrett's esophagus and overall digestive health.

Benefits include decreased pain and swelling, improved healing, and better gut health. Foods like fatty fish and leafy greens are great examples, promoting a balanced inflammatory response.

Examples of Low-Acid Foods

Examples of low-acid foods include bananas, oatmeal, spinach, and cucumbers. These foods are less likely to trigger acid reflux or exacerbate Barrett's esophagus symptoms. Bananas provide a soothing effect on the stomach lining, while oatmeal is a gentle, filling choice. Spinach and cucumbers are not only low in acid but also rich in essential nutrients that support overall health. Incorporate these foods into meals to maintain a low-acid diet.

Examples of Anti-Inflammatory Foods

Anti-inflammatory foods include salmon, walnuts, turmeric, and blueberries. Salmon is rich in omega-3 fatty acids that reduce inflammation, while walnuts provide additional omega-3s and antioxidants. Turmeric contains curcumin, which has strong anti-inflammatory properties, and blueberries are packed with antioxidants that help protect the digestive system. Including these foods in your diet can help manage inflammation associated with Barrett's esophagus.

How to Incorporate These Foods into Your Diet

Incorporate low-acid and anti-inflammatory foods by planning balanced meals. Start your day with oatmeal topped with blueberries, and have a spinach salad with salmon for lunch. Snack on bananas or walnuts throughout the day. Use turmeric in cooking to add flavor and anti-inflammatory benefits. Create a weekly meal plan that emphasizes these foods, avoiding high-acid and inflammatory ingredients like citrus and processed snacks. This approach ensures that your diet supports digestive health and reduces Barrett's esophagus symptoms.

Meal Planning and Preparation

Creating a Balanced Meal Plan

To create a balanced meal plan for managing Barrett's Esophagus, focus on low-acid, anti-inflammatory foods. Start by including lean proteins, such as chicken or fish, whole grains, and a variety of vegetables like spinach and carrots. Avoid high-fat, spicy, or acidic foods that may trigger symptoms. Plan meals to include small frequent servings to prevent overloading the stomach with too much food. For example, a typical meal could consist of baked chicken breast, quinoa, and steamed broccoli, ensuring it's easy on the digestive system while providing essential nutrients.

Grocery Shopping Tips

When shopping for Barrett's Esophagus-friendly ingredients, prioritize fresh, whole foods and avoid processed items high in acidity or fat. Choose items like low-fat dairy, non-citrus fruits (e.g., apples, bananas), and vegetables like zucchini and sweet potatoes. Avoid high-acidic foods such as tomatoes, citrus fruits, and spicy condiments. It's helpful to read labels carefully to identify hidden sources of acid or fat. For instance, opt for almond milk instead of regular milk and select plain, low-fat yogurt over flavored versions.

Essential Kitchen Tools and Equipment

For managing Barrett's Esophagus, essential kitchen tools include a blender for making smoothies and soups, a steamer for preparing vegetables, and non-stick baking sheets for cooking with less oil. Invest in measuring cups and spoons to ensure portion control and avoid high-fat ingredients. A good set of knives and a cutting board will also simplify meal preparation, making it easier to prepare low-acid, anti-inflammatory meals. For example, use a blender to make a smooth banana and oat breakfast smoothie.

Meal Prep Tips and Tricks

Meal prep for Barrett's Esophagus involves preparing and storing meals in advance to make healthy eating easier. Cook and portion out lean proteins, whole grains, and vegetables in individual containers to have ready-to-eat meals throughout the week. Use airtight containers to keep food fresh and organize meals by days of the week. Batch-cooking meals like grilled chicken and steamed vegetables can save time and reduce the temptation to reach for less suitable options. Label each container with the date and contents for easy access.

How to Adapt Recipes for Your Needs

Adapting recipes for Barrett's Esophagus involves substituting high-acid ingredients with low-acid alternatives and adjusting seasonings. Replace citrus juices with low-acid vinegar or broth, and use herbs like basil and parsley instead of spicy seasonings. For instance, if a recipe calls for tomatoes, you can use butternut squash or pumpkin as a substitute. Adjust portion sizes to avoid overeating and choose cooking methods like baking or steaming that require less fat and are gentler on the digestive system.

Chapters 1

Breakfast Ideas for Barrett's Esophagus

Low-Acid Smoothies and Juices

For Barrett's Esophagus, opt for low-acid smoothies and juices that soothe the digestive tract. Combine non-citrus fruits like bananas, pears, and melons with a base of almond milk or coconut water. Blend in a handful of spinach for added nutrients without acidity. For example, a banana-spinach smoothie involves blending 1 banana, 1 cup of spinach, 1 cup of almond milk, and a spoonful of honey. This mix is gentle on the stomach and reduces acid reflux symptoms.

Oatmeal and Whole Grain Options

Start your day with oatmeal or whole grain options that are gentle on the digestive system. Prepare oatmeal using rolled oats and water or a non-dairy milk to reduce acidity. Add mild fruits like blueberries or apples for flavor. For a simple breakfast, cook 1 cup of oats in 2 cups of water or almond milk, and top with 1/2 cup of fresh blueberries and a sprinkle of cinnamon. Whole grains like brown rice or quinoa are also beneficial, providing fiber without aggravating reflux.

Egg-Based Breakfasts

Egg-based breakfasts are excellent for managing Barrett's Esophagus when cooked without excessive fat or spice. Scramble eggs with vegetables like spinach or bell peppers, and cook using a non-stick pan with a small amount of olive oil. For instance, scramble 2 eggs with 1/2 cup of chopped spinach and a pinch of salt. Serve with whole-grain toast for a balanced, non-acidic meal that supports digestive health.

Low-Acid Fruit Combinations

Incorporate low-acid fruits into your diet to avoid triggering acid reflux. Combine fruits such as melons, pears, and bananas to create soothing fruit salads. For a refreshing option, mix 1 cup of diced cantaloupe, 1/2 cup of sliced pears, and 1/2 banana in a bowl. This combination is gentle on the stomach and provides essential nutrients without increasing acid levels.

Simple Breakfast Recipes

Simple breakfast recipes for Barrett's Esophagus should be easy to prepare and gentle on the stomach. Opt for meals like whole-grain toast with almond butter or a bowl of oatmeal with a splash of almond milk. For a quick recipe, toast 2 slices of whole-grain bread and spread 1 tablespoon of almond butter on each. This straightforward breakfast is low in acid and provides lasting energy without discomfort.

Chapters 2

Lunch Recipes for Digestive Health

Low-Acid Soups and Stews

For managing Barrett's esophagus, choose soups and stews with low-acid ingredients like butternut squash, sweet potatoes, and carrots. A simple recipe involves simmering diced butternut squash with vegetable broth, onions, and garlic until tender. Blend until smooth for a creamy texture. Avoid tomatoes, citrus, and spicy seasonings, which can trigger reflux. Opt for herbs like basil or thyme for flavor.

Grilled Vegetables and Salads

Grill non-acidic vegetables such as zucchini, bell peppers, and eggplant. Brush them lightly with olive oil and season with herbs like rosemary and oregano. Grilled vegetables can be a nutritious addition to salads. Combine with a base of spinach or kale, and dress with a mild vinaigrette made from olive oil and a touch of honey. Avoid vinegar-based dressings and raw onions, which can be irritating.

Lean Protein Options

Incorporate lean proteins like skinless chicken breast, turkey, or fish. For a straightforward meal, bake chicken breasts seasoned with a sprinkle of garlic powder and a dash of salt. Serve with steamed vegetables or a side of quinoa. These proteins are easy on the digestive system and less likely to trigger acid reflux compared to higher-fat meats.

Whole Grain and Vegetable Combos

Combine whole grains like brown rice or quinoa with cooked vegetables for a balanced meal. A simple dish could be quinoa mixed with steamed broccoli, carrots, and a small amount of olive oil. This combination provides fiber and essential nutrients while being gentle on the stomach. Avoid adding acidic or spicy sauces.

Easy Lunch Recipes

Prepare easy, Barrett's-friendly lunches like a turkey and spinach wrap. Use a whole wheat tortilla, spread a thin layer of hummus, add slices of lean turkey, and a handful of fresh spinach. Roll up and slice into pinwheels for a convenient, low-acid meal. Avoid spicy condiments or high-fat ingredients that can exacerbate symptoms.

Chapters 3

Dinner Dishes to Soothe the Digestive System

Low-Acid Main Courses

For managing Barrett's esophagus, opt for main courses low in acidity to prevent irritation. Choose lean proteins like chicken or turkey, and incorporate non-citrus vegetables such as spinach and zucchini. For instance, a grilled chicken breast with steamed broccoli and quinoa provides a soothing meal that avoids acidic triggers. Avoid tomatoes and citrus-based sauces, and instead use herbs like basil and parsley for flavoring.

Anti-Inflammatory Dinner Sides

Include anti-inflammatory sides to support digestive health and reduce inflammation. Foods such as sweet potatoes, carrots, and green beans are excellent choices. A simple side dish could be roasted sweet potato cubes with a drizzle of olive oil and a sprinkle of turmeric. These ingredients help soothe the digestive tract while providing essential nutrients without exacerbating reflux symptoms.

Healthy Cooking Methods

Use gentle cooking methods that preserve nutrients and avoid added fat. Steaming, baking, and grilling are ideal techniques. For example, steaming vegetables like carrots and green beans keeps them tender and nutrient-rich without the use of excess oil or spices. Baking fish with a light coating of herbs can also be a healthy and flavorful choice that minimizes reflux risk.

Recipe Variations and Tips

Adapt recipes to suit a low-acid, anti-inflammatory diet by substituting high-acid ingredients with suitable alternatives. For example, replace lemon juice in dressings with apple cider vinegar, and use almond or coconut milk instead of regular dairy. When preparing dishes, always taste and adjust seasoning to ensure it remains flavorful while keeping acidity low.

Simple Dinner Recipes

Prepare easy, Barrett's-friendly dinners with minimal effort. Try a quinoa salad with grilled chicken, cucumber, and avocado. Toss with a mild olive oil dressing. Another option is a baked sweet potato topped with a dollop of plain Greek yogurt and fresh herbs. These recipes are straightforward, requiring minimal ingredients while adhering to dietary needs for managing Barrett's esophagus.

Chapters 4

Snacks and Small Meals

Low-Acid Snack Options

When managing Barrett's esophagus, choosing low-acid snacks is crucial to avoid irritation. Opt for options like fresh vegetables such as carrots and cucumbers, and whole grains like oatmeal or brown rice cakes. Unsweetened applesauce and bananas are gentle on the stomach and can be soothing. Avoid citrus fruits, tomatoes, and spicy foods, as they can exacerbate acid reflux. For a quick snack, try a handful of almonds or a slice of whole-grain bread with avocado, which are both low in acid and beneficial for digestive health.

Anti-Inflammatory Snack Recipes

Anti-inflammatory snacks can help manage Barrett's esophagus by reducing irritation. Try making a chia seed pudding with almond milk, a spoonful of honey, and a dash of cinnamon. This combination offers anti-inflammatory benefits while being easy on the stomach. Another option is a smoothie made with spinach, a small amount of pineapple (which is low-acid compared to other fruits), and flaxseeds. These snacks support overall digestive health and help to combat inflammation.

Nutritious and Satisfying Snacks

To keep snacks both nutritious and satisfying, focus on incorporating protein and fiber. Greek yogurt with a drizzle of honey and a sprinkle of flaxseeds provides protein and healthy fats. Hummus with sliced cucumbers or bell peppers makes for a filling, nutrient-dense option. These snacks offer a balance of macronutrients while being easy on the digestive system. Choose whole grains, lean proteins, and plenty of vegetables to maintain energy levels and support digestive health.

Tips for Healthy Snacking

Healthy snacking involves selecting options that won't trigger acid reflux. Opt for snacks that are low in fat and acid, and avoid eating large portions. Eating smaller, frequent snacks can help keep acid levels balanced. Additionally, include snacks with soluble fiber like oats or apples to aid digestion. Drinking water or herbal teas between meals can also help soothe the digestive tract. Always listen to your body and adjust your choices based on how you feel.

Easy Snack Recipes

For quick and easy Barrett's esophagus-friendly snacks, consider preparing a batch of quinoa salad with chopped cucumbers, shredded carrots, and a light vinaigrette made from olive oil and lemon juice. Another simple recipe is baked sweet potato fries seasoned with a pinch of paprika. These snacks are not only easy to make but also provide essential nutrients while minimizing acid reflux triggers. Keep pre-cut vegetables and fruits handy for convenient snacking options throughout the day.

Chapters 5

Desserts That Won't Irritate

Low-Acid Dessert Recipes

For those managing Barrett's Esophagus, choosing desserts with low-acid ingredients is crucial. Opt for recipes using fruits like bananas or apples, and avoid citrus or tomatoes. A simple option is baked apples with a sprinkle of cinnamon, which is gentle on the stomach. Another choice is a chia seed pudding made with almond milk, which soothes and doesn't trigger acid reflux. These desserts provide comfort without exacerbating symptoms.

Anti-Inflammatory Ingredients for Sweets

Incorporating anti-inflammatory ingredients into desserts can help manage Barrett's Esophagus symptoms. Use turmeric, ginger, and cinnamon to add flavor and health benefits. For example, a turmeric-infused almond milk latte can be a soothing treat. Additionally, using coconut oil instead of butter can reduce inflammation. These ingredients not only help reduce inflammation but also make desserts more digestive-friendly.

Fruit-Based Desserts

Fruit-based desserts can be a great option if you choose low-acid fruits. Try a fruit salad featuring pears, peaches, and berries. Another option is a baked pear dessert where pears are baked with a touch of honey and cinnamon. These desserts are naturally sweet and less likely to irritate the esophagus compared to higher-acid fruits.

Nut and Seed Desserts

Nuts and seeds are excellent for low-acid diets and provide a satisfying crunch. Recipes like almond flour cookies or chia seed energy balls can be both delicious and gentle on your stomach. For instance, making almond butter balls with a pinch of vanilla and a small amount of honey offers a creamy, satisfying dessert that doesn't trigger acid reflux.

Simple Dessert Ideas

Simple desserts that are easy on the stomach include oatmeal cookies made with rolled oats, banana, and a touch of honey. Another easy idea is a smoothie made with non-citrus fruits like apples or peaches, blended with almond milk and a spoonful of flaxseeds.

Chapters 6

Beverages for Barrett's Esophagus

Low-Acid Smoothies and Juices

Low-acid smoothies and juices are essential for managing Barrett's esophagus and reducing acid reflux. Use non-citrus fruits like bananas, pears, and melons as the base. Blend these with low-fat yogurt or almond milk to create a smooth, creamy texture that is gentle on your digestive system. For example, a banana and pear smoothie can be made by blending one banana, one pear, and a cup of almond milk. Avoid adding acidic fruits like oranges or strawberries.

Herbal Teas and Infusions

Herbal teas and infusions can soothe the digestive tract and help manage Barrett's esophagus symptoms. Opt for non-caffeinated, low-acid herbs such as chamomile, ginger, and licorice root. Brew a cup of chamomile tea by steeping one chamomile tea bag in hot water for 5 minutes. Ginger can be made into an infusion by boiling fresh ginger slices in water for 10 minutes. These options provide relief without irritating the esophagus.

Hydrating Drinks

Hydrating drinks help maintain overall digestive health and reduce acid reflux. Water is the best choice, but you can also include coconut water and aloe vera juice. For a refreshing option, try mixing coconut water with a splash of low-acid fruit juice, such as apple juice. Aim to drink 6-8 glasses of water daily to stay hydrated and support digestion.

Recipes for Homemade Beverages

Creating homemade beverages allows you to control ingredients and avoid triggers. For a soothing drink, blend 1 cup of unsweetened almond milk with 1 tablespoon of honey and a pinch of ground cinnamon. For a hydrating cucumber-mint cooler, blend 1 cucumber with a handful of fresh mint leaves and a cup of water. Strain and serve chilled for a refreshing, low-acid beverage.

Tips for Choosing the Right Beverages

When selecting beverages for Barrett's esophagus, focus on those with low acidity and no caffeine. Avoid carbonated drinks and citrus juices that can exacerbate symptoms. Look for drinks labeled as "non-acidic" or "pH-balanced" to ensure they are gentle on the digestive system. Always check ingredient lists to avoid added sugars or artificial flavors that could trigger acid reflux.

Chapters 7

Managing Acid Reflux with Food

Foods That Help Reduce Acid Reflux

Opt for low-acid and alkaline foods to minimize acid reflux. Examples include bananas, melons, oatmeal, and leafy greens. These foods help neutralize stomach acid and reduce irritation in the esophagus. For a practical approach, start your day with a bowl of oatmeal topped with banana slices, and include leafy greens like spinach in your lunch salads to balance acidity. Drinking herbal teas such as chamomile can also soothe the digestive tract.

Recipes to Alleviate Symptoms

Prepare meals that incorporate soothing ingredients to ease Barrett's Esophagus symptoms. A simple recipe to try is a creamy butternut squash soup: blend cooked butternut squash with low-sodium chicken broth, a touch of olive oil, and a pinch of ginger. This recipe is mild, soothing, and anti-inflammatory. Another option is a quinoa salad with cucumbers, avocados, and a light lemon-olive oil dressing. These recipes are designed to be gentle on the stomach while providing essential nutrients.

How to Combine Foods for Optimal Results

Combining foods that are low in acid and high in fiber can enhance digestive health and reduce reflux symptoms. For instance, pairing oatmeal with a handful of almonds or combining grilled chicken with steamed vegetables can create a balanced meal that supports digestion. Avoid mixing high-fat foods with acidic ones; instead, focus on whole grains, lean proteins, and non-citrus fruits to maintain a stable pH balance in the stomach.

Foods to Avoid and Why

Avoid foods that trigger acid reflux or irritation. This includes spicy foods, citrus fruits, tomatoes, and caffeinated beverages. These items increase stomach acid production or irritate the esophagus lining. For example, limit your intake of orange juice and spicy dishes like chili, which can exacerbate symptoms. Opt for milder alternatives like herbal teas and non-citrus fruits such as pears.

Practical Tips for Daily Management

Implement daily habits to manage Barrett's Esophagus effectively. Eat smaller, more frequent meals instead of large ones to reduce stomach pressure. Avoid lying down immediately after eating; wait at least two to three hours to prevent acid from traveling back up the esophagus. Elevate the head of your bed if nighttime reflux is an issue. Additionally, stay hydrated with water and herbal teas, and maintains a healthy weight to reduce pressure on the stomach.

Chapters 8

Incorporating Anti-Inflammatory Foods

Anti-Inflammatory Meal Ideas

To manage Barrett's Esophagus and reduce acid reflux, focus on meals that incorporate anti-inflammatory ingredients. Opt for dishes like quinoa salad with roasted vegetables and a lemon-tahini dressing, which provide nutrients without irritating the esophagus. Prepare soothing turmeric and ginger tea or a sweet potato and spinach stew.

These options are gentle on the digestive system and help reduce inflammation. For breakfast, try oatmeal with blueberries and a sprinkle of chia seeds to start your day with a low-acid, anti-inflammatory boost

Recipes Featuring Key Ingredients

Create meals using key anti-inflammatory ingredients such as ginger, turmeric, and leafy greens. For example, a ginger-turmeric chicken soup combines anti-inflammatory spices with lean protein and vegetables. Another option is a spinach and avocado smoothie, blending spinach (rich in antioxidants) with avocado (for healthy fats). Incorporate these ingredients into your recipes to not only reduce inflammation but also enhance overall digestive health, making your meals both therapeutic and delicious.

Benefits of Anti-Inflammatory Diet

An anti-inflammatory diet helps alleviate symptoms of Barrett's Esophagus by reducing irritation and promoting healing. Consuming low-acid, anti-inflammatory foods can lower acid reflux occurrences, soothe the esophagus lining, and improve digestive comfort. This diet also supports overall gut health, reduces inflammation-related discomfort, and may help prevent complications associated with Barrett's Esophagus by calming the digestive tract.

How to Balance with Other Dietary Needs

To balance an anti-inflammatory diet with other dietary needs, consider incorporating variety while avoiding triggers. For those with gluten intolerance, use gluten-free grains like rice or quinoa. If dairy is a concern, opt for plant-based milk alternatives. Ensure your meals are still nutrient-dense by including a variety of vegetables, lean proteins, and healthy fats. This way, you maintain an anti-inflammatory approach while meeting specific dietary restrictions or preferences.

Sample Meal Plans

Design meal plans that adhere to anti-inflammatory principles while accommodating your daily routine. For instance, a daily plan might include a breakfast of chia pudding with berries, a lunch of grilled chicken with quinoa and steamed broccoli, and a dinner of baked salmon with sweet potato mash. Include snacks like apple slices with almond butter or a handful of walnuts. Adjust portion sizes based on your needs and ensure each meal balances anti-inflammatory benefits with nutritional adequacy.

Chapters 9

Tips for Adapting Recipes and Meal Planning

Adjusting Recipes for Individual Tastes

When adjusting recipes for Barrett's esophagus, tailor the flavors and ingredients to suit individual preferences while maintaining low-acid and anti-inflammatory guidelines. Use herbs like basil and oregano to enhance taste without adding acidity. Substitute spicy or acidic ingredients like tomatoes and citrus with milder options such as roasted vegetables or fresh herbs.

Experiment with different spices and seasoning blends to create satisfying dishes that don't compromise digestive comfort. For instance, if a recipe calls for lemon juice, replace it with a splash of apple cider vinegar mixed with water for a milder tang.

Planning for Special Occasions

For special occasions, create Barrett's-friendly meals by focusing on low-acid, anti-inflammatory dishes that feel festive yet gentle on the digestive system. Prepare dishes like herb-roasted chicken with a side of quinoa and steamed green beans, which are both soothing and celebratory. Opt for desserts made with non-citrus fruits, such as a baked apple with a cinnamon sprinkle. Use garnishes like fresh herbs to add visual appeal and flavor without triggering reflux. Plan ahead by testing recipes and adjusting seasonings to ensure they align with dietary needs.

Budget-Friendly Meal Planning

To plan budget-friendly meals for Barrett's esophagus, focus on cost-effective ingredients that meet dietary restrictions. Buy in-season vegetables, whole grains, and lean proteins in bulk to save money. Utilize versatile ingredients like sweet potatoes, which can be used in multiple recipes such as soups, stews, or baked dishes. Make homemade versions of store-bought items like sauces and dressings, using low-acid and anti-inflammatory ingredients. Plan weekly menus and create a shopping list based on sales and seasonal produce to keep costs down while maintaining a nutritious diet.

Managing Dietary Changes over Time

Successfully managing dietary changes for Barrett's esophagus involves gradual adjustments and continuous monitoring. Start by incorporating one new low-acid food at a time and observe its impact on symptoms. Keep a food diary to track which ingredients work well and which ones should be avoided. Adjust recipes as needed based on feedback from your digestive system and make note of any recurring issues. Consult with a nutritionist periodically to reassess dietary needs and ensure that any changes are still aligned with maintaining digestive health.

Resources for Ongoing Support

For ongoing support in managing Barrett's esophagus, utilize resources such as online forums, dietary blogs, and support groups dedicated to digestive health. Access reputable websites that offer recipes, tips, and advice for managing acid reflux and inflammation. Consider joining local or online cooking classes focused on Barrett's-friendly diets to learn new techniques and recipes. Engage with healthcare professionals who can provide personalized advice and updates on the latest research. Keeping up with these resources will help you stay informed and motivated in your dietary management.

Chapters 10

Common Concerns and FAQs

Common Dietary Challenges

Managing Barrett's esophagus requires avoiding trigger foods that exacerbate acid reflux. Common challenges include limiting spicy foods, citrus fruits, and fatty items that can increase acid production. To handle these, focus on a diet rich in low-acid, anti-inflammatory foods such as leafy greens, lean proteins, and whole grains. Practical adjustments involve substituting acidic ingredients with milder options—such as using non-citrus fruits like apples or pears in place of oranges—and preparing meals using methods like baking or steaming rather than frying.

How to Handle Eating Out

Eating out with Barrett's esophagus can be tricky, but preparation helps. Opt for restaurants that offer customizable menus where you can request adjustments to avoid trigger ingredients. When ordering, choose dishes that are grilled or steamed rather than fried, and ask for dressings and sauces on the side.

Examples include requesting plain grilled chicken instead of fried and substituting high-acidic sauces with olive oil or vinegar-based dressings. It's also wise to communicate your dietary needs clearly to the staff to ensure your meal meets your dietary restrictions.

Managing Flare-Ups and Symptoms

To manage flare-ups, it's essential to identify and avoid personal trigger foods and follow a balanced, low-acid diet. Implement lifestyle changes such as eating smaller, more frequent meals and avoiding eating late at night to reduce symptoms. During a flare-up, focus on soothing foods like oatmeal, bananas, and almond milk, which are less likely to irritate the esophagus. Keeping a food diary can also help track what triggers symptoms and adjust your diet accordingly.

Adapting Recipes for Family Meals

Adapting recipes to accommodate Barrett's esophagus while still catering to family preferences involves modifying ingredients and cooking techniques. Replace acidic or spicy components with milder alternatives and use herbs like basil and thyme instead of chili powder. For instance, in a family-friendly pasta dish, swap out tomato-based sauces for a creamy, non-acidic sauce made with low-fat yogurt or pureed vegetables. This ensures that meals are both Barrett's-friendly and enjoyable for everyone.

Where to Find Additional Resources and Support

For additional support, explore resources such as online forums, local support groups, and educational websites dedicated to Barrett's esophagus and digestive health. Organizations like the American Gastroenterological Association offer valuable information and guidance. Additionally, consulting with a registered dietitian who specializes in digestive disorders can provide personalized advice and meal planning. Books and cookbooks focused on managing Barrett's esophagus can also offer practical recipes and tips to support dietary changes.

BONUSES

30 days Delicious Recipes,

14 days Snacks,

14 days Beverages and

14 days Smoothies

Following these sequences:

Ingredients Needed

Tools Needed

Cooking and Prep Times

Step-By-Step Instructions on Its Preparation

Number of Servings

Ingredients Needed:

- 2 large sweet potatoes
- 2 tablespoons olive oil
- 1 teaspoon ground cumin
- 1/2 teaspoon smoked paprika
- 1/2 teaspoon garlic powder
- Salt to taste (optional)
- Pepper to taste (optional)

Tools Needed:

- Baking sheet
- Parchment paper
- Mandoline slicer or sharp knife
- Mixing bowl
- Brush for oil
- Oven

Cooking and Prep Times:

Prep Time: 15 minutes

Cooking Time: 25 minutes

Total Time: 40 minutes

Step-by-Step Instructions on Its Preparation:

- **Preheat Oven:** First heat your oven to a temperature of 400°F (200°C). Line a baking sheet with parchment paper.

- **Prepare Sweet Potatoes:** Peel the sweet potatoes and slice them thinly (about 1/8-inch thick) using a mandoline slicer or a sharp knife.

- **Season:** In a mixing bowl, toss the sweet potato slices with olive oil, ground cumin, smoked paprika, garlic powder, salt, and pepper until evenly coated.

- **Arrange on Baking Sheet:** Spread the sweet potato slices in a single layer on the prepared baking sheet. Make sure they are not overlapping to ensure they crisp up evenly.

- **Bake:** Bake in the preheated oven for about 25 minutes, or until the chips are golden brown and crispy. Flip the chips halfway through baking for even crispness.

- **Cool:** Allow the chips to cool on the baking sheet for a few minutes before serving.

Number of Servings:

Approximately 4 servings

Snack: Apple Slices with Almond Butter

Ingredients Needed:

- 1 large apple
- 2 tablespoons almond butter (smooth or crunchy)

Tools Needed:

- Knife
- Apple corer (optional)
- Plate

Prep Time:

5 minutes

Step-by-Step Instructions on Its Preparation:

Prepare Apple: Wash and core the apple. Slice it into wedges.

Serve: Arrange the apple slices on a plate and serve with almond butter for dipping.

Number of Servings:

1 serving (for individual consumption)

Beverage: Ginger Mint Herbal Tea

Ingredients Needed:

- 1 teaspoon dried ginger root
- 1 teaspoon dried mint leaves
- 2 cups boiling water

Tools Needed:

- Teapot or heatproof container
- Strainer

Prep Time:

5 minutes **Steeping Time:**

10 minutes

Step-by-Step Instructions on Its Preparation:

- **Combine Ingredients:** Place the dried ginger root and dried mint leaves in a teapot or heatproof container.
- **Add Water:** Pour boiling water over the herbs.
- **Steep:** Let the tea steep for 10 minutes.

- **Strain and Serve:** Strain the tea into cups and serve warm.

Number of Servings:

2 servings

Smoothie: Banana Spinach Smoothie

Ingredients Needed:

- 1 ripe banana
- 1 cup fresh spinach leaves
- 1/2 cup unsweetened almond milk
- 1/2 cup plain Greek yogurt
- 1 tablespoon honey (optional)

Tools Needed:

- Blender
- Measuring cups
- Spoon

Prep Time:

5 minutes

Step-by-Step Instructions on Its Preparation:

Combine Ingredients: Place the banana, spinach leaves, almond milk, Greek yogurt, and honey (if using) in a blender.

Blend: Blend until smooth and creamy.

Serve: Pour into a glass and serve immediately.

Number of Servings:

1 serving

Week 1: Day 2

Recipe Name: Roasted Chickpeas

Ingredients Needed:

- 1 can (15 oz) chickpeas, drained and rinsed
- 1 tablespoon olive oil
- 1 teaspoon paprika
- 1/2 teaspoon turmeric
- 1/2 teaspoon garlic powder
- Salt to taste

Tools Needed:

- Baking sheet

- Parchment paper
- Mixing bowl
- Oven

Cooking and Prep Times:

Prep Time: 10 minutes

Cooking Time: 25 minutes

Total Time: 35 minutes

Step-by-Step Instructions on Its Preparation:

- **Preheat Oven:** First heat your oven to a temperature of 400°F (200°C). Line a baking sheet with parchment paper.
- **Prepare Chickpeas:** Pat the chickpeas dry with a paper towel.
- **Season:** In a mixing bowl, toss the chickpeas with olive oil, paprika, turmeric, garlic powder, and salt.
- **Roast:** Spread the chickpeas in a single layer on the baking sheet. Bake for 25 minutes, stirring halfway through, until they are crispy.
- **Cool:** Let the chickpeas cool before serving.

Number of Servings:

Approximately 4 servings

Snack: Carrot Sticks with Hummus

Ingredients Needed:

- 2 large carrots
- 1/2 cup hummus

Tools Needed:

- Knife
- Peeler
- Plate

Prep Time:

5 minutes

Step-by-Step Instructions on Its Preparation:

Prepare Carrots:

Serve: Arrange the carrot sticks on a plate with hummus for dipping.

Number of Servings:

1 serving (for individual consumption)

Beverage: Chamomile Tea

Ingredients Needed:

- 1 chamomile tea bag
- 1 cup boiling water

Tools Needed:

- Teacup
- Kettle or pot

Prep Time:

5 minutes **Steeping Time:**

5 minutes

Step-by-Step Instructions on Its Preparation:

Boil Water: Boil water in a kettle or pot.

Steep Tea: Place the chamomile tea bag in a teacup and pour boiling water over it. Let steep for 5 minutes.

Serve: Remove the tea bag and serve warm.

Number of Servings:

1 serving

Smoothie: Blueberry Almond Smoothie

Ingredients Needed:

- 1/2 cup frozen blueberries
- 1/2 cup unsweetened almond milk
- 1/4 cup almond butter
- 1 tablespoon chia seeds
- 1 teaspoon honey (optional)

Tools Needed:

- Blender
- Measuring cups
- Spoon

Prep Time:

5 minutes

Step-by-Step Instructions on Its Preparation:

- **Combine Ingredients:** Place the frozen blueberries, almond milk, almond butter, chia seeds, and honey (if using) in a blender.
- **Blend:** Blend until smooth.

Serve: Pour into a glass and serve immediately.

Number of Servings:

1 serving

Week 1: Day 3

Recipe Name: Quinoa Salad with Cucumber and Dill

Ingredients Needed:

- 1 cup cooked quinoa
- 1 cucumber, diced
- 1/4 cup chopped fresh dill
- 2 tablespoons olive oil
- 1 tablespoon lemon juice
- Salt and pepper to taste

Tools Needed:

- Mixing bowl
- Spoon
- Knife

Cooking and Prep Times:

Prep Time: 10 minutes

Cooking Time: 15 minutes (for quinoa)

Total Time: 25 minutes

Step-by-Step Instructions on Its Preparation:

- **Cook Quinoa:** Cook quinoa according to package instructions and let it cool.
- **Mix Ingredients:** In a mixing bowl, combine the cooked quinoa, diced cucumber, and chopped dill.
- **Dress Salad:** Drizzle it properly with olive oil and some lemon juice. Season with salt and pepper.
- **Toss and Serve:** Toss everything together and serve.

Number of Servings:

Approximately 4 servings

Snack: Celery Sticks with Greek Yogurt Dip

Ingredients Needed:

- 3 celery stalks
- 1/2 cup plain Greek yogurt
- 1 tablespoon lemon juice
- 1 teaspoon dried dill

Tools Needed:

- Knife
- Mixing bowl
- Spoon
- Plate

Prep Time:

5 minutes

Step-by-Step Instructions on Its Preparation:

Prepare Celery: Cut celery stalks into sticks.

Make Dip: In a mixing bowl, combine Greek yogurt, lemon juice, and dried dill.

Serve: Arrange celery sticks on a plate with the yogurt dip for dipping.

Number of Servings:

1 serving (for individual consumption)

Beverage: Peppermint Tea

Ingredients Needed:

- 1 peppermint tea bag

- 1 cup boiling water

Tools Needed:

- Teacup
- Kettle or pot

Prep Time:

5 minutes **Steeping Time:**

5 minutes

Step-by-Step Instructions on Its Preparation:

Boil Water: Boil water in a kettle or pot.

Steep Tea: Place the peppermint tea bag in a teacup and pour boiling water over it. Let steep for 5 minutes.

Serve: Remove the tea bag and serve warm.

Number of Servings:

1 serving

Smoothie: Spinach Pineapple Smoothie

Ingredients Needed:

- 1 cup fresh spinach leaves
- 1/2 cup frozen pineapple chunks

- 1/2 cup unsweetened coconut milk
- 1 tablespoon flaxseeds

Tools Needed:

Blender

Measuring cups

Spoon

Prep Time:

5 minutes

Step-by-Step Instructions on Its Preparation:

- **Combine Ingredients:** Place spinach leaves, pineapple chunks, coconut milk, and flaxseeds in a blender.
- **Blend:** Blend until smooth and creamy.
- **Serve:** Pour into a glass and serve immediately.

Number of Servings:

1 serving

Recipe Name: Baked Apple Slices with Cinnamon

Ingredients Needed:

- 2 large apples
- 1 tablespoon olive oil
- 1 teaspoon ground cinnamon
- 1 tablespoon honey (optional)

Tools Needed:

- Baking sheet
- Parchment paper
- Knife
- Mixing bowl
- Oven

Cooking and Prep Times:

Prep Time: 10 minutes

Cooking Time: 20 minutes

Total Time: 30 minutes

Step-by-Step Instructions on Its Preparation:

Preheat Oven: First heat your oven to a temperature of 350°F (175°C). Line a baking sheet with parchment paper.

Prepare Apples: Core and slice apples into thin rounds.

Season: In a mixing bowl, toss apple slices with olive oil and ground cinnamon. Drizzle with honey if desired.

Arrange on Baking Sheet: Spread apple slices in a single layer on the baking sheet.

Bake: Bake for 20 minutes or until the apple slices are tender and slightly caramelized.

Cool: Let cool before serving.

Number of Servings:

Approximately 4 servings

Snack: Cucumber Slices with Avocado Dip

Ingredients Needed:

- 1 cucumber
- 1 ripe avocado
- 1 tablespoon lime juice
- Salt and pepper to taste

Tools Needed:

- Knife
- Spoon
- Mixing bowl
- Plate

Prep Time:

10 minutes

Step-by-Step Instructions on Its Preparation:

Prepare Cucumber: Slice cucumber into thin rounds.

Make Dip: In a mixing bowl, mash the avocado and mix in lime juice, salt, and pepper.

Serve: Arrange cucumber slices on a plate with avocado dip for dipping.

Number of Servings:

1 serving (for individual consumption)

Beverage: Rooibos Tea

Ingredients Needed:

- 1 Rooibos tea bag

- 1 cup boiling water

Tools Needed:

- Teacup
- Kettle or pot

Prep Time:

5 minutes **Steeping Time:**

5 minutes

Step-by-Step Instructions on Its Preparation:

- **Boil Water:** Boil water in a kettle or pot.
- **Steep Tea:** Place the rooibos tea bag in a teacup and pour boiling water over it. Let steep for 5 minutes.
- **Serve:** Remove the tea bag and serve warm.

Number of Servings:

1 serving

Smoothie: Strawberry Banana Smoothie

Ingredients Needed:

- 1 cup frozen strawberries

- 1 banana
- 1/2 cup plain yogurt
- 1/2 cup unsweetened almond milk
- 1 teaspoon honey (optional)

Tools Needed:

- Blender
- Measuring cups
- Spoon

Prep Time:

5 minutes

Step-by-Step Instructions on Its Preparation:

Combine Ingredients: Place strawberries, banana, yogurt, almond milk, and honey (if using) in a blender.

Blend: Blend until smooth.

Serve: Pour into a glass and serve immediately.

Number of Servings:

1 serving

Recipe Name: Zucchini Chips

Ingredients Needed:

- 2 medium zucchinis
- 2 tablespoons olive oil
- 1/2 teaspoon dried oregano
- 1/4 teaspoon garlic powder
- Salt to taste

Tools Needed:

- Baking sheet
- Parchment paper
- Mandoline slicer or knife
- Oven

Cooking and Prep Times:

Prep Time: 15 minutes

Cooking Time: 20 minutes

Total Time: 35 minutes

Step-by-Step Instructions on Its Preparation:

- **Preheat Oven:** First heat your oven to a temperature of 375°F (190°C). Line a baking sheet with parchment paper.
- **Prepare Zucchini:** Slice the zucchinis into thin rounds using a mandoline slicer or knife.
- **Season:** Toss zucchini slices with olive oil, dried oregano, garlic powder, and salt in a mixing bowl.
- **Arrange on Baking Sheet:** Spread the zucchini slices in a single layer on the baking sheet.
- **Bake:** Bake for 20 minutes, flipping the slices halfway through, until they are crispy.
- **Cool:** Let cool before serving.

Number of Servings:

Approximately 4 servings

Snack: Bell Pepper Strips with Guacamole

Ingredients Needed:

- 1 red bell pepper
- 1/2 cup guacamole

Tools Needed:

- Knife
- Plate

Prep Time:

5 minutes

Step-by-Step Instructions on Its Preparation:

- **Prepare Bell Pepper:** Slice the bell pepper into strips.
- **Serve:** Arrange the bell pepper strips on a plate with guacamole for dipping.

Number of Servings:

1 serving (for individual consumption)

Beverage: Warm Lemon Water

Ingredients Needed:

- 1 lemon
- 1 cup warm water

Tools Needed:

- Mug
- Knife

- Juicer (optional)

Prep Time:

5 minutes

Step-by-Step Instructions on Its Preparation:

- **Juice Lemon:** Squeeze the juice of half a lemon into a mug.
- **Add Water:** Fill the mug with warm water and stir.

Serve: Serve warm.

Number of Servings:

1 serving

Smoothie: Mango Kale Smoothie

Ingredients Needed:

- 1/2 cup frozen mango chunks
- 1 cup fresh kale leaves
- 1/2 cup coconut water
- 1/4 cup plain Greek yogurt
- 1 tablespoon chia seeds

Tools Needed:

- Blender
- Measuring cups
- Spoon

Prep Time:

5 minutes

Step-by-Step Instructions on Its Preparation:

- **Combine Ingredients:** Place mango chunks, kale leaves, coconut water, Greek yogurt, and chia seeds in a blender.
- **Blend:** Blend until smooth and creamy.

Serve: Pour into a glass and serve immediately.

Number of Servings:

1 serving

Week 1: Day 6

Recipe Name: Roasted Butternut Squash

Ingredients Needed:

- 1 small butternut squash
- 2 tablespoons olive oil

- 1/2 teaspoon ground cinnamon
- 1/4 teaspoon nutmeg
- Salt to taste

Tools Needed:

- Baking sheet
- Parchment paper
- Knife
- Oven

Cooking and Prep Times:

Prep Time: 15 minutes

Cooking Time: 30 minutes

Total Time: 45 minutes

Step-by-Step Instructions on Its Preparation:

- **Preheat Oven:** First heat your oven to a temperature of 400°F (200°C). Line a baking sheet with parchment paper.
- **Prepare Squash:**
- **Season:** Toss the squash cubes with olive oil, ground cinnamon, nutmeg, and salt in a mixing bowl.

- **Arrange on Baking Sheet:** Spread the squash cubes in a single layer on the baking sheet.
- **Roast:** Roast for 30 minutes, or until tender and slightly caramelized, stirring halfway through.
- **Cool:** Let cool before serving.

Number of Servings:

Approximately 4 servings

Snack: Sliced Pear with Cottage Cheese

Ingredients Needed:

- 1 ripe pear
- 1/2 cup low-fat cottage cheese

Tools Needed:

- Knife
- Plate

Prep Time:

5 minutes

Step-by-Step Instructions on Its Preparation:

Prepare Pear: Slice the pear into wedges.

Serve: Arrange the pear slices on a plate with cottage cheese.

Number of Servings:

1 serving (for individual consumption)

Beverage: Herbal Ginger Tea

Ingredients Needed:

- 1 teaspoon dried ginger root
- 1 cup boiling water

Tools Needed:

- Teacup
- Kettle or pot
- Strainer

Prep Time:

5 minutes **Steeping Time:**

5 minutes

Step-by-Step Instructions on Its Preparation:

- **Combine Ingredients:** Place the dried ginger root in a teacup.

- **Add Water:** Pour boiling water over the ginger.
- **Steep:** Let steep for 5 minutes.
- **Strain and Serve:** Strain the tea into a cup and serve warm.

Number of Servings:

1 serving

Smoothie: Avocado Pineapple Smoothie

Ingredients Needed:

- 1/2 avocado
- 1/2 cup frozen pineapple chunks
- 1/2 cup unsweetened almond milk
- 1 tablespoon honey (optional)

Tools Needed:

- Blender
- Measuring cups
- Spoon

Prep Time:

5 minutes

Step-by-Step Instructions on Its Preparation:

- **Combine Ingredients:** Place avocado, pineapple chunks, almond milk, and honey (if using) in a blender.

- **Blend:** Blend until smooth.

Serve: Pour into a glass and serve immediately.

Number of Servings:

1 serving

Week 1: Day 7

Recipe Name: Steamed Green Beans

Ingredients Needed:

- 1 pound fresh green beans
- 1 tablespoon olive oil
- 1/2 teaspoon garlic powder
- Salt to taste

Tools Needed:

- Steamer basket
- Pot
- Mixing bowl

- Plate

Cooking and Prep Times:

Prep Time: 10 minutes

Cooking Time: 10 minutes

Total Time: 20 minutes

Step-by-Step Instructions on Its Preparation:

- **Prepare Green Beans:**
- **Steam:** Place the green beans in a steamer basket over boiling water. Steam for about 10 minutes, or until tender-crisp.
- **Season:** Toss the steamed green beans with olive oil, garlic powder, and salt in a mixing bowl.

Serve: Transfer to a plate and serve.

Number of Servings:

Approximately 4 servings

Snack: Almonds and Dried Cranberries

Ingredients Needed:

- 1/4 cup raw almonds

- 1/4 cup dried cranberries (unsweetened)

Tools Needed:

- Small bowl

Prep Time:

5 minutes

Step-by-Step Instructions on Its Preparation:

- **Combine Ingredients:** Place almonds and dried cranberries in a small bowl.
- **Serve:** Serve as a snack.

Number of Servings:

1 serving (for individual consumption)

Beverage: Fennel Tea

Ingredients Needed:

- 1 teaspoon fennel seeds
- 1 cup boiling water

Tools Needed:

- Teacup
- Kettle or pot

- Strainer

Prep Time:

5 minutes **Steeping Time:**

5 minutes

Step-by-Step Instructions on Its Preparation:

- **Combine Ingredients:** Place fennel seeds in a teacup.
- **Add Water:** Pour boiling water over the seeds.
- **Steep:** Let steep for 5 minutes.
- **Strain and Serve:** Strain the tea into a cup and serve warm.

Number of Servings:

1 serving

Smoothie: Kiwi Spinach Smoothie

Ingredients Needed:

- 2 kiwis, peeled
- 1 cup fresh spinach leaves
- 1/2 cup coconut water
- 1/4 cup plain Greek yogurt

Tools Needed:

- Blender
- Measuring cups
- Spoon

Prep Time:

5 minutes

Step-by-Step Instructions on Its Preparation:

- **Combine Ingredients:** Place kiwis, spinach leaves, coconut water, and Greek yogurt in a blender.
- **Blend:** Blend until smooth and creamy.

Serve: Pour into a glass and serve immediately.

Number of Servings:

1 serving

Week 2: Day 1

Recipe Name: Quinoa Salad with Avocado

Ingredients Needed:

- 1 cup cooked quinoa

- 1 avocado, diced
- 1 cup cherry tomatoes, halved
- 1/2 cucumber, diced
- 1/4 cup chopped fresh parsley
- 2 tablespoons olive oil
- 1 tablespoon lemon juice
- Salt and pepper to taste

Tools Needed:

- Mixing bowl
- Knife
- Cutting board
- Measuring spoons

Cooking and Prep Times:

Prep Time: 10 minutes

Cooking Time: 0 minutes (assuming quinoa is pre-cooked)

Total Time: 10 minutes

Step-by-Step Instructions on Its Preparation:

- **Combine Ingredients:** In a mixing bowl, combine the cooked quinoa, diced avocado, cherry tomatoes, cucumber, and parsley.
- **Prepare Dressing:** In a small bowl, whisk together olive oil, lemon juice, salt, and pepper.
- **Mix Salad:** Pour the dressing over the quinoa mixture and toss gently to combine.

Serve: Serve immediately or chill before serving.

Number of Servings:

2 servings

Snack: Carrot Sticks with Hummus

Ingredients Needed:

- 2 large carrots
- 1/2 cup hummus (store-bought or homemade)

Tools Needed:

- Knife
- Peeler
- Plate

Prep Time:

5 minutes

Step-by-Step Instructions on Its Preparation:

- **Prepare Carrots:** Peel and cut the carrots into sticks.
- **Serve:** Arrange carrot sticks on a plate with hummus for dipping.

Number of Servings:

1 serving (for individual consumption)

Beverage: Peppermint Tea

Ingredients Needed:

- 1 peppermint tea bag
- 1 cup boiling water

Tools Needed:

- Teacup
- Kettle or pot

Prep Time:

5 minutes **Steeping Time:**

5 minutes

Step-by-Step Instructions on Its Preparation:

- **Steep Tea:** Place the peppermint tea bag in a teacup and pour boiling water over it.
- **Steep:** Let steep for 5 minutes.

Serve: Remove the tea bag and serve warm.

Number of Servings:

1 serving

Smoothie: Berry Spinach Smoothie

Ingredients Needed:

- 1/2 cup frozen mixed berries
- 1 cup fresh spinach leaves
- 1/2 banana
- 1 cup unsweetened almond milk

Tools Needed:

- Blender
- Measuring cups

Prep Time:

5 minutes

Step-by-Step Instructions on Its Preparation:

- **Combine Ingredients:** Place berries, spinach, banana, and almond milk in a blender.
- **Blend:** Blend until smooth.

Serve: Pour into a glass and serve immediately.

Number of Servings:

1 serving

Week 2: Day 2

Recipe Name: Steamed Broccoli with Lemon

Ingredients Needed:

- 1 head of broccoli
- 1 tablespoon olive oil
- 1 tablespoon lemon juice
- 1/2 teaspoon garlic powder
- Salt and pepper to taste

Tools Needed:

- Steamer basket

- Pot
- Mixing bowl
- Plate

Cooking and Prep Times:

Prep Time: 10 minutes

Cooking Time: 10 minutes

Total Time: 20 minutes

Step-by-Step Instructions on Its Preparation:

- **Prepare Broccoli:** Wash and cut the broccoli properly into florets.
- **Steam:** Place the broccoli florets in a steamer basket over boiling water. Steam for about 10 minutes or until tender.
- **Season:** Toss steamed broccoli with olive oil, lemon juice, garlic powder, salt, and pepper in a mixing bowl.
- **Serve:** Transfer to a plate and serve.

Number of Servings:

4 servings

Snack: Apple Slices and little Almond Butter

Ingredients Needed:

1 apple

2 tablespoons almond butter

Tools Needed:

- Knife
- Plate

Prep Time:

5 minutes

Step-by-Step Instructions on Its Preparation:

Prepare Apple: Slice the apple into wedges.

Serve: Arrange apple slices on a plate with almond butter for dipping.

Number of Servings:

1 serving (for individual consumption)

Beverage: Chamomile Tea

Ingredients Needed:

- 1 chamomile tea bag
- 1 cup boiling water

Tools Needed:

- Teacup
- Kettle or pot

Prep Time:

5 minutes **Steeping Time:**

5 minutes

Step-by-Step Instructions on Its Preparation:

Steep Tea: Place the chamomile tea bag in a teacup and pour boiling water over it.

Steep: Let steep for 5 minutes.

Serve: Remove the tea bag and serve warm.

Number of Servings:

1 serving

Smoothie: Pineapple Coconut Smoothie

Ingredients Needed:

- 1/2 cup frozen pineapple chunks
- 1/2 cup coconut milk
- 1/2 banana
- 1 tablespoon chia seeds

Tools Needed:

- Blender
- Measuring cups

Prep Time:

5 minutes

Step-by-Step Instructions on Its Preparation:

Combine Ingredients: Place pineapple chunks, coconut milk, banana, and chia seeds in a blender.

Blend: Blend until smooth.

Serve: Pour into a glass and serve immediately.

Number of Servings:

1 serving

Recipe Name: Cucumber Mint Salad

Ingredients Needed:

- 1 cucumber
- 1/4 cup chopped fresh mint
- 2 tablespoons olive oil
- 1 tablespoon red wine vinegar
- Salt and pepper to taste

Tools Needed:

- Knife
- Cutting board
- Mixing bowl

Cooking and Prep Times:

- Prep Time: 10 minutes
- Cooking Time: 0 minutes
- Total Time: 10 minutes

Step-by-Step Instructions on Its Preparation:

Prepare Cucumber: Peel and slice the cucumber into thin rounds.

Mix Ingredients: In a mixing bowl, combine cucumber slices, chopped mint, olive oil, red wine vinegar, salt, and pepper.

Serve: Toss to coat and serve immediately.

Number of Servings:

2 servings

Snack: Celery Sticks with Peanut Butter

Ingredients Needed:

- 2 celery stalks
- 2 tablespoons peanut butter (smooth or chunky)

Tools Needed:

Knife

Plate

Prep Time:

5 minutes

Step-by-Step Instructions on Its Preparation:

- **Prepare Celery:** Cut the celery stalks into sticks.

- **Serve:** Arrange celery sticks on a plate with peanut butter for dipping.

Number of Servings:

1 serving (for individual consumption)

Beverage: Ginger Lemonade

Ingredients Needed:

- 1 tablespoon freshly grated ginger
- 1 tablespoon lemon juice
- 1 cup cold water
- 1 teaspoon honey (optional)

Tools Needed:

- Glass
- Spoon
- Strainer (optional)

Prep Time:

5 minutes

Step-by-Step Instructions on Its Preparation:

- **Combine Ingredients:** In a glass, combine ginger, lemon juice, and cold water. Stir well.

- **Sweeten:** Add honey if desired, and stir again.
- **Serve:** Serve chilled.
- **Number of Servings:**
- 1 serving

Smoothie: Green Apple Spinach Smoothie

Ingredients Needed:

- 1 green apple, cored and sliced
- 1 cup fresh spinach
- 1/2 cup unsweetened almond milk
- 1/4 cup Greek yogurt

Tools Needed:

- Blender
- Measuring cups

Prep Time:

5 minutes

Step-by-Step Instructions on Its Preparation:

Combine Ingredients: Place green apple slices, spinach, almond milk, and Greek yogurt in a blender.

Blend: Blend until smooth.

Serve: Pour into a glass and serve immediately.

Number of Servings:

1 serving

Week 2: Day 4

Recipe Name: Baked Sweet Potato Fries

Ingredients Needed:

- 2 large sweet potatoes
- 2 tablespoons olive oil
- 1/2 teaspoon paprika
- 1/2 teaspoon garlic powder
- Salt to taste

Tools Needed:

- Baking sheet
- Parchment paper
- Knife
- Oven

Cooking and Prep Times:

Prep Time: 15 minutes

Cooking Time: 25 minutes

Total Time: 40 minutes

Step-by-Step Instructions on Its Preparation:

- **Preheat Oven:** First heat your oven to a temperature of 400°F (200°C). Line a baking sheet with parchment paper.
- **Prepare Sweet Potatoes:** Peel and cut the sweet potatoes into thin strips.
- **Season:** Toss the sweet potato strips with olive oil, paprika, garlic powder, and salt in a mixing bowl.
- **Arrange on Baking Sheet:** Spread the strips in a single layer on the prepared baking sheet.
- **Bake:** Bake for 20-25 minutes, turning halfway through, until crispy and golden brown.

Serve: Let cool slightly before serving.

Number of Servings:

4 servings

Snack: Sliced Pear with Cottage Cheese

Ingredients Needed:

- 1 pear

- 1/2 cup low-fat cottage cheese

Tools Needed:

- Knife
- Plate

Prep Time:

5 minutes

Step-by-Step Instructions on Its Preparation:

Prepare Pear: Slice the pear into wedges.

Serve: Arrange pear slices on a plate with cottage cheese.

Number of Servings:

1 serving (for individual consumption)

Beverage: Herbal Chamomile Tea

Ingredients Needed:

- 1 chamomile tea bag
- 1 cup boiling water

Tools Needed:

- Teacup
- Kettle or pot

Prep Time:

5 minutes **Steeping Time:**

5 minutes

Step-by-Step Instructions on Its Preparation:

- **Steep Tea:** Place the chamomile tea bag in a teacup and pour boiling water over it.
- **Steep:** Let steep for 5 minutes.
- **Serve:** Remove the tea bag and serve warm.
- **Number of Servings:**
- 1 serving

Smoothie: Strawberry Banana Smoothie

Ingredients Needed:

- 1/2 cup frozen strawberries
- 1/2 banana
- 1/2 cup unsweetened almond milk
- 1 tablespoon flaxseeds

Tools Needed:

- Blender
- Measuring cups

Prep Time:

5 minutes

Step-by-Step Instructions on Its Preparation:

- **Combine Ingredients:** Place strawberries, banana, almond milk, and flaxseeds in a blender.
- **Blend:** Blend until smooth.

Serve: Pour into a glass and serve immediately.

Number of Servings:

1 serving

Week 2: Day 5

Recipe Name: Roasted Brussels Sprouts

Ingredients Needed:

- 1 pound Brussels sprouts
- 2 tablespoons olive oil
- 1/2 teaspoon dried thyme
- 1/2 teaspoon garlic powder
- Salt and pepper to taste

Tools Needed:

- Baking sheet
- Parchment paper
- Knife
- Oven

Cooking and Prep Times:

Prep Time: 10 minutes

Cooking Time: 25 minutes

Total Time: 35 minutes

Step-by-Step Instructions on Its Preparation:

- **Preheat Oven:** First heat your oven to a temperature of 400°F (200°C). Line a baking sheet with parchment paper.
- **Prepare Brussels Sprouts:** Trim and halve the Brussels sprouts.
- **Season:** Toss the Brussels sprouts with olive oil, thyme, garlic powder, salt, and pepper.
- **Arrange on Baking Sheet:** Spread the Brussels sprouts in a single layer on the prepared baking sheet.

- **Roast:** Roast for 20-25 minutes, or until crispy and browned.

Serve: Serve immediately.

Number of Servings:

4 servings

Snack: Greek Yogurt with Blueberries

Ingredients Needed:

- 1 cup plain Greek yogurt
- 1/2 cup fresh blueberries

Tools Needed:

- Bowl
- Spoon

Prep Time:

5 minutes

Step-by-Step Instructions on Its Preparation:

Combine Ingredients: Place Greek yogurt in a bowl and top with fresh blueberries.

Serve: Enjoy immediately.

Number of Servings:

1 serving (for individual consumption)

Beverage: Aloe Vera Juice

Ingredients Needed:

- 1/2 cup aloe vera juice
- 1/2 cup water

Tools Needed:

- Glass
- Spoon

Prep Time:

5 minutes

Step-by-Step Instructions on Its Preparation:

- **Mix Ingredients:** Combine aloe vera juice and water in a glass.
- **Serve:** Stir and serve chilled.

Number of Servings:

1 serving

Smoothie: Mango Kale Smoothie

Ingredients Needed:

- 1/2 cup frozen mango chunks
- 1 cup fresh kale leaves
- 1/2 banana
- 1 cup coconut water

Tools Needed:

- Blender
- Measuring cups

Prep Time:

5 minutes

Step-by-Step Instructions on Its Preparation:

Combine Ingredients: Place mango, kale, banana, and coconut water in a blender.

Blend: Blend until smooth.

Serve: Pour into a glass and serve immediately.

Number of Servings:

1 serving

Recipe Name: Spaghetti Squash with Tomato Basil Sauce

Ingredients Needed:

- 1 medium spaghetti squash
- 1 cup tomato sauce (low-acid)
- 1/4 cup fresh basil, chopped
- 1 tablespoon olive oil
- Salt and pepper to taste

Tools Needed:

- Baking sheet
- Knife
- Oven
- Saucepan

Cooking and Prep Times:

Prep Time: 15 minutes

Cooking Time: 45 minutes

Total Time: 1 hour

Step-by-Step Instructions on Its Preparation:

- **Preheat Oven:** First heat your oven to a temperature of 400°F (200°C).
- **Prepare Squash:** Cut the spaghetti squash in half lengthwise and remove the seeds.
- **Bake:** Place the squash halves cut-side down on a baking sheet and bake for 40-45 minutes, or until tender.
- **Prepare Sauce:** While the squash is baking, heat the tomato sauce in a saucepan over medium heat. Stir in chopped basil and cook for 5 minutes.
- **Scrape Squash:** Once the squash is baked, use a fork to scrape the flesh into strands.
- **Combine:** Top the squash with tomato basil sauce and serve.

Number of Servings:

4 servings

Snack: Cucumber Slices with Guacamole

Ingredients Needed:

- 1 cucumber
- 1/2 cup guacamole (store-bought or homemade)

Tools Needed:

- Knife
- Plate

Prep Time:

5 minutes

Step-by-Step Instructions on Its Preparation:

- **Prepare Cucumber:** Slice the cucumber into rounds.
- **Serve:** Arrange cucumber slices on a plate with guacamole for dipping.

Number of Servings:

1 serving (for individual consumption)

Beverage: Herbal Ginger Tea

Ingredients Needed:

- 1 tablespoon fresh ginger, sliced
- 1 cup boiling water

Tools Needed:

- Teacup

- Kettle or pot

Prep Time:

5 minutes **Steeping Time:**

5 minutes

Step-by-Step Instructions on Its Preparation:

- **Prepare Ginger:** Place ginger slices in a teacup.
- **Steep:** Pour boiling water over the ginger and let steep for 5 minutes.

Serve: Strain and serve warm.

Number of Servings:

1 serving

Smoothie: Kiwi Pineapple Smoothie

Ingredients Needed:

- 1 kiwi, peeled
- 1/2 cup pineapple chunks
- 1/2 cup coconut water
- 1/2 banana

Tools Needed:

- Blender
- Measuring cups

Prep Time:

5 minutes

Step-by-Step Instructions on Its Preparation:

- **Combine Ingredients:** Place kiwi, pineapple, coconut water, and banana in a blender.
- **Blend:** Blend until smooth.

Serve: Pour into a glass and serve immediately.

Number of Servings:

1 serving

Week 2: Day 7

Recipe Name: Cauliflower Rice with Herbs

Ingredients Needed:

1 head of cauliflower

- 2 tablespoons olive oil
- 1/4 cup fresh parsley, chopped
- 1/4 cup fresh chives, chopped

- Salt and pepper to taste

Tools Needed:

- Food processor or grater
- Pan
- Knife
- Cutting board

Cooking and Prep Times:

Prep Time: 10 minutes

Cooking Time: 10 minutes

Total Time: 20 minutes

Step-by-Step Instructions on Its Preparation:

- **Prepare Cauliflower:** Remove the leaves and stem from the cauliflower and cut into florets. Use a food processor or grater to process the cauliflower into rice-sized pieces.
- **Cook:** Heat olive oil in a pan over medium heat. Add the cauliflower rice and boil it properly for about 5-7 minutes, stirring occasionally.
- **Add Herbs:** Stir in parsley, chives, salt, and pepper, and cook for an additional 2-3 minutes.

Serve: Serve warm as a side dish.

Number of Servings:

4 servings

Snack: Almonds and Dried Cranberries

Ingredients Needed:

- 1/4 cup raw almonds
- 1/4 cup dried cranberries (unsweetened)

Tools Needed:

Bowl

Prep Time:

2 minutes

Step-by-Step Instructions on Its Preparation:

Combine Ingredients: Place almonds and dried cranberries in a bowl.

Serve: Enjoy as a quick snack.

Number of Servings:

1 serving (for individual consumption)

Beverage: Mint Lemonade

Ingredients Needed:

- 1 lemon, juiced
- 1 tablespoon fresh mint leaves
- 1 cup cold water
- 1 teaspoon honey (optional)

Tools Needed:

- Glass
- Spoon

Prep Time:

5 minutes

Step-by-Step Instructions on Its Preparation:

Combine Ingredients: Mix lemon juice, fresh mint leaves, cold water, and honey (if using) in a glass.

Serve: Stir well and serve chilled.

Number of Servings:

1 serving

Smoothie: Berry Spinach Smoothie

Ingredients Needed:

- 1/2 cup mixed berries (fresh or frozen)
- 1 cup fresh spinach
- 1/2 banana
- 1/2 cup almond milk

Tools Needed:

- Blender
- Measuring cups

Prep Time:

5 minutes

Step-by-Step Instructions on Its Preparation:

Combine Ingredients: Place mixed berries, spinach, banana, and almond milk in a blender.

Blend: Blend until smooth.

Serve: Pour into a glass and serve immediately.

Number of Servings:

1 serving

Recipe Name: Quinoa Salad with Cucumbers and Bell Peppers

Ingredients Needed:

- 1 cup quinoa
- 2 cups water
- 1 cup diced cucumber
- 1 cup diced red bell pepper
- 1/4 cup chopped fresh parsley
- 2 tablespoons olive oil
- 1 tablespoon lemon juice
- Salt and pepper to taste

Tools Needed:

- Saucepan
- Mixing bowl
- Knife
- Cutting board

Cooking and Prep Times:

- Prep Time: 10 minutes
- Cooking Time: 15 minutes

- Total Time: 25 minutes

Step-by-Step Instructions on Its Preparation:

- **Cook Quinoa:** Rinse quinoa under cold water. In a pan, bring 2 cups of water and boil it. Add quinoa, reduce heat, cover, and simmer for 15 minutes or until water is absorbed and quinoa is tender. Fluff with a fork and let cool.

- **Prepare Vegetables:** While the quinoa is cooking, dice the cucumber and red bell pepper. Chop the parsley.

- **Combine Ingredients:** In a large mixing bowl, combine the cooked quinoa, cucumber, bell pepper, and parsley.

- **Dress Salad:** Drizzle it properly with olive oil and some lemon juice. Season with salt and pepper

- **Serve:** Toss gently to mix and serve.

Number of Servings:

4 servings

Recipe Name: Baked Sweet Potatoes with Spinach and Feta

Ingredients Needed:

- 4 medium sweet potatoes
- 2 cups fresh spinach
- 1/2 cup crumbled feta cheese
- 2 tablespoons olive oil
- Salt and pepper to taste

Tools Needed:

- Baking sheet
- Parchment paper
- Knife
- Oven

Cooking and Prep Times:

Prep Time: 10 minutes

Cooking Time: 40 minutes

Total Time: 50 minutes

Step-by-Step Instructions on Its Preparation:

- **Preheat Oven:** First heat your oven to a temperature of 400°F (200°C). Line a baking sheet with parchment paper.

- **Prepare Sweet Potatoes:** Wash and pierce sweet potatoes with a fork. Place them on the baking sheet.

- **Bake:** Bake for 35-40 minutes, or until tender.

- **Prepare Spinach:** While sweet potatoes are baking, sauté spinach in olive oil until wilted.

- **Assemble:** Once sweet potatoes are done, let cool slightly. Slice open and fluff with a fork. Top with sautéed spinach and crumbled feta. Season with salt and pepper.

Serve: Serve warm.

Number of Servings:

4 servings

Recipe Name: Lentil and Vegetable Stew

Ingredients Needed:

- 1 cup dried green or brown lentils
- 1 tablespoon olive oil
- 1 onion, chopped
- 2 carrots, diced
- 2 celery stalks, diced
- 2 cloves garlic, minced
- 1 can (14.5 oz) diced tomatoes
- 4 cups vegetable broth
- 1 teaspoon dried thyme
- 1 bay leaf
- Salt and pepper to taste

Tools Needed:

- Large pot
- Knife
- Cutting board
- Wooden spoon

Cooking and Prep Times:

Prep Time: 10 minutes

Cooking Time: 40 minutes

Total Time: 50 minutes

Step-by-Step Instructions on Its Preparation:

- **Prepare Lentils:** Rinse lentils under cold water. Set aside.
- **Sauté Vegetables:** In a pot, heat the oil over a low heat. Add onion, carrots, and celery. Sauté for like 5-7 minutes.
- **Add Garlic:** Stir in minced garlic and cook for 1 minute.

Add Lentils and Liquid: Add lentils, diced tomatoes, vegetable broth, thyme, and bay leaf. Bring to a boil.

Simmer: Reduce heat and simmer for 30-35 minutes, or until lentils and vegetables are tender. Remove bay leaf.

Season:

Serve: Serve hot.

Number of Servings:

4 servings

Recipe Name: Stuffed Bell Peppers

Ingredients Needed:

- 4 large bell peppers (any color)
- 1 cup cooked brown rice
- 1 cup black beans, drained and rinsed
- 1/2 cup corn kernels
- 1/2 cup diced tomatoes
- 1/4 cup chopped cilantro
- 1 teaspoon cumin

Salt and pepper to taste

Tools Needed:

- Baking dish
- Knife
- Oven
- Mixing bowl

Cooking and Prep Times:

Prep Time: 15 minutes

Cooking Time: 30 minutes

Total Time: 45 minutes

Step-by-Step Instructions on Its Preparation:

- **Preheat Oven:** First heat your oven to a temperature of 375°F (190°C).
- **Prepare Peppers:** Slice the tops off the bell peppers and remove seeds and membranes. Place them in a baking dish.
- **Prepare Filling:** In a mixing bowl, combine cooked brown rice, black beans, corn, diced tomatoes, cilantro, cumin, salt, and pepper.
- **Stuff Peppers:** Spoon the filling into each bell pepper.
- **Bake:** Cover with foil and bake for 25-30 minutes, until peppers are tender.

Serve: Serve warm.

Number of Servings:

4 servings

Recipe Name: Zucchini Noodles with Tomato Basil Sauce

Ingredients Needed:

- 3 medium zucchinis
- 1 cup tomato sauce (low-acid)
- 1/4 cup fresh basil, chopped
- 2 tablespoons olive oil
- Salt and pepper to taste

Tools Needed:

- Spiralizer or vegetable peeler
- Pan
- Knife
- Cutting board

Cooking and Prep Times:

Prep Time: 10 minutes

Cooking Time: 10 minutes

Total Time: 20 minutes

Step-by-Step Instructions on Its Preparation:

- **Prepare Zucchini:** Use a spiralizer or vegetable peeler to make zucchini noodles.
- **Cook Zucchini:** Heat olive oil in a pan over medium heat. Add zucchini noodles and cook for 3-5 minutes until slightly tender.
- **Add Sauce:** Stir in tomato sauce and cook for an additional 5 minutes.
- **Add Basil:** Stir in fresh basil and season with salt and pepper.

Serve: Serve immediately.

Number of Servings:

4 servings

Week 3: Day 6

Recipe Name: Chicken and Vegetable Stir-Fry

Ingredients Needed:

- 1 pound boneless, skinless chicken breast, thinly sliced
- 2 tablespoons olive oil
- 1 cup broccoli florets
- 1 cup sliced bell peppers

- 1 cup snap peas
- 2 tablespoons low-sodium soy sauce
- 1 tablespoon rice vinegar
- 1 teaspoon grated ginger
- Salt and pepper to taste

Tools Needed:

- Large skillet or wok
- Knife
- Cutting board

Cooking and Prep Times:

Prep Time: 15 minutes

Cooking Time: 15 minutes

Total Time: 30 minutes

Step-by-Step Instructions on Its Preparation:

- **Cook Chicken:** Heat olive oil in a large skillet or wok over medium-high heat. Add sliced chicken and cook until no longer pink, about 5-7 minutes.
- **Add Vegetables:** Add broccoli, bell peppers, and snap peas to the skillet.

- **Add Sauce:** Stir in soy sauce, rice vinegar, and grated ginger. Cook for an additional 2 minutes.
- **Season:** Season with salt and pepper to taste.

Serve: Serve warm.

Number of Servings:

4 servings

Week 3: Day 7

Recipe Name: Baked Cod with Lemon and Herbs

Ingredients Needed:

- 4 cod fillets (about 6 oz each)
- 2 tablespoons olive oil
- 1 lemon, sliced
- 2 tablespoons fresh parsley, chopped
- 1 teaspoon dried oregano
- Salt and pepper to taste

Tools Needed:

- Baking dish
- Knife

- Oven

Cooking and Prep Times:

Prep Time: 10 minutes

Cooking Time: 20 minutes

Total Time: 30 minutes

Step-by-Step Instructions on Its Preparation:

- **Preheat Oven:** First heat your oven to a temperature of 375°F (190°C).
- **Prepare Cod:** Place cod fillets in the baking dish. Drizzle with olive oil and season with salt, pepper, oregano, and chopped parsley.
- **Add Lemon:** Top each fillet with lemon slices.
- **Bake:** Bake for about 15-20 minutes, or probably until the fish is opaque and flakes easily with a fork.

Serve: Serve warm.

Number of Servings:

4 servings

Ingredients Needed:

- 1 head cauliflower, cut into florets
- 1 can (15 oz) chickpeas, drained and rinsed
- 1 tablespoon olive oil
- 1 onion, chopped
- 2 cloves garlic, minced
- 1 tablespoon curry powder
- 1 can (14.5 oz) diced tomatoes
- 1 cup coconut milk
- Salt and pepper to taste

Tools Needed:

- Large pot
- Knife
- Cutting board
- Wooden spoon

Cooking and Prep Times:

Prep Time: 15 minutes

Cooking Time: 30 minutes

Total Time: 45 minutes

Step-by-Step Instructions on Its Preparation:

- **Sauté Onion and Garlic:** Heat olive oil in a large pot over medium heat. Add onion and cook it well until it is soft, like about 5 minutes. Stir in garlic and cook for an additional minute.
- **Add Spices:** Add curry powder and cook for 1 minute.
- **Add Vegetables and Liquid:** Add cauliflower florets, chickpeas, diced tomatoes, and coconut milk. Bring to a boil.
- **Simmer:** Reduce heat and simmer for 20-25 minutes, or until cauliflower is tender.
- **Season:** Season with salt and pepper to taste.

Serve: Serve warm.

Number of Servings:

4 servings

Recipe Name: Turkey and Spinach Stuffed Mushrooms

Ingredients Needed:

- 12 large mushrooms, stems removed
- 1/2 pound ground turkey
- 1 cup fresh spinach, chopped
- 1/4 cup grated Parmesan cheese
- 1 clove garlic, minced
- 1 tablespoon olive oil
- Salt and pepper to taste

Tools Needed:

- Baking sheet
- Pan
- Knife
- Oven

Cooking and Prep Times:

Prep Time: 15 minutes

Cooking Time: 25 minutes

Total Time: 40 minutes

Step-by-Step Instructions on Its Preparation:

- **Preheat Oven:** First heat your oven to a temperature of 375°F (190°C). Lightly grease a baking sheet.
- **Cook Turkey:** Heat olive oil in a pan over medium heat. Add ground turkey and cook until browned. Stir in minced garlic and spinach, cooking until spinach is wilted.
- **Stuff Mushrooms:** Mix cooked turkey and spinach with Parmesan cheese. Stuff mixture into mushroom caps.
- **Bake:** Place stuffed mushrooms on the baking sheet and bake for 20-25 minutes, or until mushrooms are tender.

Serve: Serve warm.

Number of Servings:

4 servings

Recipe Name: Sweet Potato and Black Bean Tacos

Ingredients Needed:

- 2 large sweet potatoes, peeled and diced
- 1 can (15 oz) black beans, drained and rinsed
- 1 tablespoon olive oil
- 1 teaspoon cumin
- 1/2 teaspoon paprika
- Salt and pepper to taste
- 8 small corn tortillas
- Fresh cilantro, for garnish

Tools Needed:

- Baking sheet
- Pan
- Knife
- Oven

Cooking and Prep Times:

Prep Time: 10 minutes

Cooking Time: 25 minutes

Total Time: 35 minutes

Step-by-Step Instructions on Its Preparation:

- **Preheat Oven:** First heat your oven to a temperature of 400°F (200°C). Line a baking sheet with parchment paper.
- **Roast Sweet Potatoes:** Toss diced sweet potatoes with olive oil, cumin, paprika, salt, and pepper. Spread on the baking sheet and roast for 20-25 minutes, or until tender.
- **Warm Beans:** Heat black beans in a pan over medium heat.
- **Assemble Tacos:** Warm tortillas according to package instructions in the label. Fill with roasted sweet potatoes and black beans. Garnish with fresh cilantro.

Serve: Serve warm.

Number of Servings:

4 servings

Recipe Name: Baked Eggplant Parmesan

Ingredients Needed:

- 1 large eggplant, sliced into 1/4-inch rounds
- 1 cup whole wheat breadcrumbs
- 1/2 cup grated Parmesan cheese
- 1 cup marinara sauce (low-acid)
- 1 cup shredded mozzarella cheese
- 2 tablespoons olive oil
- Salt and pepper to taste

Tools Needed:

- Baking sheet
- Parchment paper
- Oven
- Knife

Cooking and Prep Times:

Prep Time: 20 minutes

Cooking Time: 30 minutes

Total Time: 50 minutes

Step-by-Step Instructions on Its Preparation:

- **Preheat Oven:** First heat your oven to a temperature of 375°F (190°C). Line a baking sheet with parchment paper.

- **Prepare Eggplant:** Brush eggplant slices with olive oil and season with salt and pepper. Place on the baking sheet.

- **Bake Eggplant:** Bake for 20 minutes, turning halfway through.

- **Assemble Dish:** Spread a layer of marinara sauce on the bottom of a baking dish. Arrange baked eggplant slices on top. Sprinkle with Parmesan cheese and shredded mozzarella.

- **Bake:** Bake for an additional 10 minutes, until cheese is melted and bubbly.

Serve: Serve warm.

Number of Servings:

4 servings

Ingredients Needed:

- 1 can (15 oz) chickpeas, drained and rinsed
- 1 cup cherry tomatoes, halved
- 1 cucumber, diced
- 1/2 cup kalamata olives, pitted
- 1/4 cup red onion, thinly sliced
- 1/4 cup crumbled feta cheese
- 2 tablespoons olive oil
- 1 tablespoon red wine vinegar
- 1 teaspoon dried oregano
- Salt and pepper to taste

Tools Needed:

- Mixing bowl
- Knife
- Cutting board

Cooking and Prep Times:

Prep Time: 10 minutes

Cooking Time: 0 minutes

Total Time: 10 minutes

Step-by-Step Instructions on Its Preparation:

- **Combine Ingredients:** In a mixing bowl, combine chickpeas, cherry tomatoes, cucumber, olives, red onion, and feta cheese.
- **Dress Salad:** Drizzle with olive oil and red wine vinegar. Sprinkle with oregano, salt, and pepper.

Serve: Toss gently and serve.

Number of Servings:

4 servings

Week 4: Day 6

Recipe Name: Roasted Chicken with Herbs

Ingredients Needed:

- 4 boneless, skinless chicken thighs
- 2 tablespoons olive oil
- 1 tablespoon fresh rosemary, chopped
- 1 tablespoon fresh thyme, chopped
- 1 lemon, quartered

- Salt and pepper to taste

Tools Needed:

- Baking dish
- Knife
- Oven

Cooking and Prep Times:

Prep Time: 10 minutes

Cooking Time: 35 minutes

Total Time: 45 minutes

Step-by-Step Instructions on Its Preparation:

Preheat Oven: First heat your oven to a temperature of 400°F (200°C). Grease a baking dish with olive oil.

- **Prepare Chicken:** Rub chicken thighs with olive oil, rosemary, thyme, salt, and pepper. Place in the baking dish.
- **Add Lemon:** Scatter lemon quarters around the chicken.
- **Bake:** Bake for 30-35 minutes, or until chicken is cooked through and reaches an internal temperature of 165°F (74°C).

Serve: Serve warm.

Number of Servings:

4 servings

Week 4: Day 7

Recipe Name: Butternut Squash Soup

Ingredients Needed:

- 1 large butternut squash, peeled and cubed
- 1 tablespoon olive oil
- 1 onion, chopped
- 2 cloves garlic, minced
- 4 cups vegetable broth
- 1/4 teaspoon nutmeg
- Salt and pepper to taste

Tools Needed:

- Large pot
- Blender or immersion blender

Knife

Cooking and Prep Times:

Prep Time: 15 minutes

Cooking Time: 30 minutes

Total Time: 45 minutes

Step-by-Step Instructions on Its Preparation:

- **Sauté Vegetables:**
- **Cook Squash:** Add butternut squash and vegetable broth.
- **Blend Soup:** Use a blender or immersion blender to puree the soup until smooth.
- **Season:** Stir in cinnamon, nutmeg, salt, and pepper.

Serve: Serve warm.

Number of Servings:

4 servings

Conclusion

In conclusion, this cookbook, *Healing Recipes for Managing Barrett's Esophagus, Reducing Acid Reflux, and Supporting Digestive Health with Low-Acid Anti-Inflammatory Foods*, offers a comprehensive approach to dietary management and digestive well-being. By meticulously following the meal plans and recipes provided, you are equipped to effectively manage Barrett's Esophagus and mitigate its associated symptoms. The carefully selected low-acid and anti-inflammatory ingredients are designed to soothe the digestive tract and promote overall health.

Adhering to these guidelines will not only assist in overcoming the challenges posed by Barrett's Esophagus but also foster a healthier, more comfortable lifestyle. Your commitment to these dietary practices is a crucial step towards achieving lasting relief and improving your quality of life. May this book serve as a valuable resource on your journey to better digestive health and wellness.

Author's appreciation

I want to extend my heartfelt gratitude to each and every one of you who has embraced my book, *Barrette Esophagus Diet Cookbook: Healing Recipes for Managing Barrett's Esophagus, Reducing Acid Reflux and Supporting Digestive Health with Low-Acid Anti-Inflammatory Foods*. Your support and enthusiasm for this guide are deeply appreciated, and it's incredibly fulfilling to know that my efforts to create a resource that truly makes a difference in managing Barrett's esophagus and improving digestive health have resonated with you.

Your commitment to adopting a diet that focuses on low-acid, anti-inflammatory foods is a powerful step toward better health. I am thrilled to see how the recipes and tips within these pages have become part of your journey toward reducing acid reflux and nurturing your digestive system.

Thank you for your trust and for sharing in this mission to support and enhance well-being through diet. Your encouragement fuels my passion for creating more resources that can make a meaningful impact. I am excited for the continued journey together as we strive for better health and digestive harmony.

Made in United States
Orlando, FL
05 December 2024

55016172R00083